Stavanger Travel Guide

Sightseeing, Hotel, Restaurant & Shopping Highlights

Sara Laing

Copyright © 2014, Astute Press
All Rights Reserved.

No part of this publication may be reproduced, stored in a retrieval system, or transmitted, in any form or by any means without the prior written permission of the publisher, nor be otherwise circulated in any form of binding or cover other than that in which it is published and without similar condition being imposed on the subsequent purchaser.

If there are any errors or omissions in copyright acknowledgements the publisher will be pleased to insert the appropriate acknowledgement in any subsequent printing of this publication.

Although we have taken all reasonable care in researching this book we make no warranty about the accuracy or completeness of its content and disclaim all liability arising from its use

Table of Contents

Stavanger 6
   Culture.. 8
   Location & Orientation.. 10
   Climate & When to Visit 12

Sightseeing Highlights.. 13
   Recommended Itineraries 13
      One Day in Stavanger 13
      Two Days in Stavanger 14
   Old Stavanger 15
   Colorful Street 16
   Stavanger Cathedral 16
   Pulpit Rock 17
   Swords in Stone 18
   MUST (MUseum Stavanger) 19
      Norwegian Canning Museum 19
      Stavanger Maritime Museum 20
      Norwegian Children's Museum 20
      Stavanger Art Museum 21
      Stavanger Museum of Natural History 22
      Ledaal 22
      Breidablikk 23
      Utstein Monastery 23
      Stavanger Museum of Cultural History 24
   Broken Column 24
   The Geopark & Norwegian Petroleum Museum 25
   Flor & Fjaere Nature Park 25
   Escape to Nature 26

Recommendations for the Budget Traveller 29
   Places to Stay 29
      Skansen Hotel 29
      Victoria Hotel 30
      Best Western Havly 30
      First Hotel Alstor 31
      Radisson Blu Royal 31
   Places to Eat 32

Flor & Fjaere Nature Park 32
Big Horn 33
Bevaremegvel 33
Harbour Café 34
Gaffel & Karaffel 34
Places to Shop 35
Bjork Birch 35
Stavanger Glassblasseri 35
Ullform 36
Kvadrat 36
Fish Market 36

Stavanger

Stavanger is a picturesque Scandanavian city located on the southwestern coast of Norway. It is the third largest city in the country and also one of the oldest in Norway having been founded in the 12th century. Surrounded by some of Norway's most dramatic natural beauty, Stavanger is a favorite with nature lovers. The city – voted the 2008 European Capital of Culture – is also one of the most vibrant cities in Norway for its festivals, nightlife, and culinary scene.

Stavanger is one of the energy capitals of Europe and is often called the Oil Capital of Norway. The city has an impressive old town of wooden houses, providing an eclectic visual mix of the old and the new.

Although the area has been inhabited for thousands of years, the first settlements in Stavanger were around 1100 when it developed into an important market town. It received the status of a city in 1125, the same year as the completion of the Stavanger Cathedral – a major tourist attraction of the city to date. In its early days, Stavanger was considered as one of the major religious centers of the region – a role that considerably declined by the 16th century. Its fortunes grew in the 19th century with the growth of the local fishing industry. In the early 20th century the city's economy was dominated by the canning industry. Today, the city is best known for its offshore oil industry and its business park which is home to more than 2500 companies! The city has one of the lowest unemployment rates in Europe, but unfortunately, it is also one of the most expensive.

Although Stavanger is one of the most cosmopolitan cities in Norway, it is also very closely linked to nature with 5 lakes and 4 fjords – an inlet of the sea in between high cliffs. The outskirts of Stavanger have some of the most dramatic rock formations in this part of Europe. Of special mention is the Pulpit Rock – one of the most visited nature attractions in Norway. Stavanger also has a number of scenic beaches for those who want a tan in the tender Norwegian summer. With well over a dozen museums it would not be wrong to call Stavanger a city of museums. Another claim to fame of Stavanger is its culinary scene – often touted as Norway's answer to the Lyon food region in France. For those visiting Stavanger with families and children, there are a number of events, attractions, and amusement parks to keep everyone entertained.

Every summer, there are over 125 cruise ships that make a stop in this coastal city, making it one of the fastest growing ports of call for cruise ships in this part of Europe. Historic heritage town, magnificent natural wonders, numerous museums, and a vibrant night scene, it is no wonder that Stavanger is growing into one of the most popular tourist destinations in Norway.

Culture

There are a numbers of events and festivals going on in Stavanger at different times of the year. Most of these celebrate the heritage and culture of the Stavanger region.

Being a major port city, many festivals in Stavanger are centered on the sea and boats. The biennial Offshore Northern Seas (ONS) exhibition is one of the biggest events (around Aug) of the city. Organized by the energy sector, the city has a number of trade shows and conferences. It is nearly impossible to get a hotel room during the days of the exhibition. Fireworks, concerts, and boat parties are usually held during the evenings.

The Gladmat Food Festival is one of the largest in the country and attracts almost all the major restaurants and chefs from in and around Stavanger. From the traditional to the quirky, and from the unknown to the popular, you can find all types of Norwegian food during this festival. Restaurants and eateries that have a successful outing with their stalls during this festival often see a huge surge in their business.

The Stavanger Vinfest is a celebration of wine and the food that goes best with it. Although not a festival in the true sense, the Vinfest sees a number of restaurants participating in this annual event and serving some of the best food and wine.

The city also celebrates literature and music. The MaiJazz Stavanger is an international jazz festival where Norwegian and international jazz artists perform in various venues across the city, including bars and restaurants. The ICMF Stavanger is an international chamber music festival that is one of the finest in the country. It attracts soloists and ensembles from Norway and from many countries in Western Europe. Kapittel is the city's festival of literature. The word literally translates to chapter, and in 2014, the city will host the Kapittel 14 – the 14th edition of the festival.

17th of May is the National Day of Norway when the whole country gets into a festive mood. Stavanger also celebrates with parades, music, and many festivities. Every year, on the Saturday closest to 5th November, Vaulen – 6 km south of Stavanger – celebrates the Guy Fawkes British Bonfire Night. The historic Gunpowder Plot is celebrated with bonfires and fireworks with the backdrop of a scenic fjord.

If you are visiting Stavanger during Christmas, do not miss the Christmas Festival in Egersund – just 70 km from Stavanger. The small town comes to life with more than 50 stall selling all kinds of Christmas gifts and monks selling Christmas drinks! The regular stores are also open beyond normal hours in keeping with the Christmas spirit.

Sports lovers also have a lot to choose from in Stavanger. There are a number of ski resorts close to Stavanger. The neighboring town of Agder-Rogaland hosts many skiing and snowboarding events. Every June, Stavanger hosts the Norway Grand Slam Beach Volleyball tournament. Stavanger and its outskirts have a number of beautiful golf courses, including the popular Sola Golfklubb. Other sports that are played in Stavanger include swimming, baseball, ice hockey, rugby, and handball. The city also has a number of scenic hiking trails which are open in the summer months.

Location & Orientation

Stavanger is located on a peninsula on the southwestern coast of Norway, less than 200 km from the southernmost tip of Norway. It is 306 km southwest from the capital Oslo. Other major cities close to Stavanger include Bergen (106 km) and the Swedish city of Gothenburg (383 km).

Stavanger is served by the Stavanger Airport, Sola, IATA: SVG; https://beta.avinor.no/en/airport/stavanger-airport/. It is about a 20 minute drive from the city center. The airport is served by a number of regular and low cost carriers like British Airways, Lufthansa, KLM, SAS, Eastern Airways, and Danish Air, connecting the coastal city with European cities that include London, Copenhagen, Amsterdam, Aberdeen, and Oslo.

There is an airport bus service connecting the city, details of which can be found at - http://www.flybussen.no/en. Taxis are also available and can be booked in advance. Some of the popular taxi companies in service include Stavanger Taxi (47 51 90 90 90), Sola Taxi (47 51 650 444), and Miljotaxi Stavanger (47 51 58 66 66). Another airport that is also used by some of the low cost carriers, namely Ryanair and Wizzair, is the Haugesund Airport, Karmoy, IATA: HAU; https://beta.avinor.no/en/airport/haugesund-airport/. The 2 hr drive from the airport to the city center can be covered through the airport coach.

Train is often a preferred means of travel to Stavanger for the scenic beauty of the route as well as for the inexpensive tickets, if bought in advance. Tickets are available 90 days before the travel date and can start from as low as kr 250 (approx €30). The train timetables and ticket details can be found at - https://www.nsb.no/en/. It should be noted that tickets for long-distance can be bought online or from the station. For local trains and short hauls, you can buy from the station, vending machine, or from the train conductor. However, if you buy a ticket from the train conductor after boarding it from a station with a ticket vending machine, then you have to pay a surcharge of kr 40!

There are a few long distance bus services to Stavanger but is not as preferred as they often turn out to be more expensive and time consuming than trains. Bus services that connect Stavanger with other domestic and foreign cities include Nor-Way - http://www.nor-way.no/, Kystbussen - https://kystbussen.no/, and Lavprisexpressen - https://kystbussen.no/.

The only international ferry service that operates from Stavanger connects the city with the Danish city of Hirtshals. It is run by Fjordline - http://www.fjordline.com/.

Once in the city, you can use the public bus service which is comfortable and reliable. Tickets cost between kr 25 and 75 depending on the zones travelled. 1-day (kr 76) and 3-day (kr 126) passes are available and are highly recommended. Taxis are available but are a very expensive option. Those who are planning to drive in to the city should strictly follow the traffic rules like wearing seat belts and keeping the headlights on. Never drink and drive in Stavanger – Norway was the first country to enact laws against DUI more than half a century ago.

Climate & When to Visit

The climate of Stavanger is categorized as maritime mild temperate. Summers are cold but comfortable while winters are near freezing. The average temperature in the summer months (Apr to Oct) reaches a high of about 18 degrees Celsius with the average low around 10 degrees. In the winter months (Nov to Mar), the average temperature reaches a high of about 3 to 4 degrees Celsius with the average low often dipping just below freezing point. Early summer months are comparatively drier, precipitation being the highest between September and December. With an average of over 150 hours of monthly sunshine in the summer months and temperatures that are much milder than the winter months, Stavanger is best visited between April and September.

Sightseeing Highlights

Recommended Itineraries

One Day in Stavanger

There is a lot to see and do in Stavanger and even a whole day is not enough to cover all the attractions of this beautiful city. Before starting the tour of the city, it is recommended to buy a day pass for the public transport that will give you the flexibility to move around quickly. Pick a map from the Tourist Center that is located right next to the Breiavatnet Lake. This is where the tour starts also. Right next to the lake is the most historic landmark of the city – the Stavanger Cathedral.

Take a guided tour of this cathedral whose age is the same as that of this city. After the tour walk northwards and you will pass the warehouses, the library, and then reach the historic clock tower – once the highest point in the city. Walking downhill will take you to the harbor area. In this area is the popular Petroleum Museum. The harbor area has a number of places from where you can grab a quick lunch. Post lunch, it is time to visit the Old Town. Take a tour of the Canning Museum and the Maritime Museum – these 2 museums highlight the growth and identity of this coastal town. If you still have time, visit the historic Rogaland Theatre located to the south of the Old Town. During this whole tour, you will come across several iron statues of a male figure – each 1.95 m tall. There are 23 statues in all and is a part of the Broken Column sculpture project. If you are looking to buy some souvenirs, visit the market square next to the Stavanger Cathedral.

Two Days in Stavanger

A 2nd day in Stavanger would allow a visit to the Preikestolen – the Pulpit Rock – one of the most visited nature attractions in Norway. Start early in the morning so that you have enough time in hand for the hike and also to avoid the crowd. You can reach the area by bus, ferry, or by driving. However, there is no transport up the hill and it may take about 2hrs for an averagely fit person to get to the top.

The climb down, a quick lunch, and the return trip to Stavanger would take up most part of the day. Visit the Culture Park in north Stavanger or the Museum of Fine Arts beside the Mosvatnet Lake to unwind.

Old Stavanger

Old Stavanger – or Gamle Stavanger to the locals – is one of the most beautiful parts of the city. It is located to the west of the Vagen where there are a number of cruise ship piers. This heritage part of town comprises of 173 wooden buildings – mostly in the form of white wooden houses – that were built in the late 18th and early 19th century. Other than these wooden houses, Old Stavanger also has the Canning Museum, the Chamber of Commerce building, the Maritime Museum, and a number of consulates.

The city of Stavanger was going through a rebuilding phase after the destruction of the World War II and there were plans to raze this old part of town. However, the City Architect Einer Heden led a singlehanded protest to preserve this old part of town. Finally, in 1956, the city voted to preserve Old Stavanger and declare it a heritage area. Old Stavanger was also one of the only 3 pilot projects in Norway during the UN Architectural Year of 1975. Today, Old Stavanger is one of the trendiest parts of the city and is regarded as one of the best conserved wood house neighborhoods of North Europe.

Colorful Street

This is one of the most vibrant streets of Norway and is located on Ovre Holmegate – right next to the harbor area. On this street, there are a number of houses that are freshly colored with a different hue giving the whole street a unique chromatic display. The idea was the brainchild of hairdresser Tom Kjorsvik and the color scheme was suggested by artist Craig Flannagan. It took shape around 2005 and today the colorful street adds to the beauty and charm of the harbor area of Stavanger. The colorful street has a number of stores and cafes making it an ideal place to wander around and relax.

Stavanger Cathedral

The Stavanger Cathedral is one of the oldest buildings in Stavanger with its date of construction coinciding with the founding of the city. It is one of the very few churches in Norway that has retained its original design and is today considered one of the historic landmarks of this coastal city.

Construction of the cathedral started in the year 1100 under the supervision of Bishop Reinald who had come from Winchester, England. The first phase of construction was completed in 1125 when Stavanger was declared a cathedral city. Having being commissioned and supervised by a bishop from England, the cathedral was constructed in an Anglo-Norman style of architecture.

It is believed that the arm of the patron saint – St Svithun – is one of the original relics in this cathedral. The cathedral received some Gothic reconstructions after it was damaged in a fire in 1272. Over the years the cathedral received minor repairs and alterations– the latest being in 1999 – but it has retained its original look from the Middle Ages. The west façade of the Cathedral is going through another major maintenance work which will be completed around 2025. This cathedral has been in constant use since the 12th century.

The Cathedral is open on all days from 11 am to 7 pm with shortened hours during the winter months.

Pulpit Rock

With nearly a quarter million visitors, this is one of the most popular tourist attractions in Norway. The Preikestolen – translating to Preacher's Pulpit – popularly known as Pulpit Rock is a 604 m high steep cliff with a flat top of about 25 m by 25 m. The unique shape of the cliff, the scenic hike, and the stunning panoramic views have made this a must visit attraction if visiting Stavanger.

The cliff is located in Forsand and can be reached through public transport from Stavanger. The best option is to take the ferry from Stavanger to Tau and then take the bus to Preikestolhytta. There are several ferries and buses throughout the day but it is recommended to reach early to avoid the crowd.

The bus stops at a short distance from the cliff. The walk up to the base of the cliff and then the hike to the top takes about 2 hrs. Do not forget to have warm clothes, water, and some packed food. Sturdy and comfortable shoes are recommended. For those who are planning to drive, follow the Rv 13 route. There is a parking fee of NOK 100 for vehicles.

The Pulpit Rock is best visited in the summer months to enjoy the clear views. In fact, the hike is closed in the winter months due to snow and severe weather. The surrounding landscape is that of the Ryfylke region with cliffs that reach up to 843 m. The landscape is dotted with beautiful lush green valleys and small lakes making the hike to the top all the more exciting and worthwhile.

Swords in Stone

The Swords in Stone is a war monument in Stavanger. It is made up of 3 huge bronze swords – each about 10 m tall – that are planted on solid rock. The monument was created by local artist Fritz Roed and was unveiled in 1983 by King Olav V. It was created in memory of the Battle of Hafrsfjord of 872 in which Harald Harfagre – also known as the Fairheaded Harald – united the kingdom of Norway. The 3 swords, with their face down in the rock, represent unification of the kingdom. It also represents eternal peace as the swords are planted solidly inside the rock as if they can never be removed. The sword which is slightly larger represents the triumphant Harald while the other 2 smaller swords represent the kings who were defeated.

The monument is located in Mollebukta – a small bay in Hafrsfjord – located on the southern outskirts of Stavanger. Mollebukta was once the site of a corn mill; today it is a popular recreational area and an often-visited tourist attraction.

MUST (MUseum Stavanger)

Museum Stavanger is a regional museum focusing on cultural history, natural history, fine arts, industrial, and maritime history. It has under it a number of museums and historic mansions. The museum was established in 1877.

Norwegian Canning Museum

This is one of the most popular museums of the city. It was established in 1975 and is housed in a refurbished cannery that was in operation between 1916 and 1958. The oldest part of the museum dates back to 1841. Canning was once the major industry in Stavanger and in the museum you can see how fishballs and canned sprats were made. Try to visit the museum on the first Sunday of the month, or on Tuesday or Thursday in the summer months when the wood-burning ovens are lit and fresh warm sardines are served using the century old machines! Located right next to the museum is the workers' cottage.

The museum is located in Old Stavanger on Ovre Strandgate 88. It is open from Tuesday to Sunday from 11 am to 4 pm.

Stavanger Maritime Museum

The Maritime Museum was established in 1926. It was originally housed in Musegt 16 but was moved to its present location in 1985. Today, the museum is housed in the Vagen quay in seafront warehouses and merchant buildings that are nearly 200 year old. This historic location on the seafront has added to the feel of the museum that explores and exhibits the development and impact of the shipping industry on this coastal port city. The highlight of the collections is the two sailboats – the mid 19th century Anna af Sand and the late 19th century Wyvern. The collection also includes 4 open boats; about 7500 artifacts related to models, maritime business, and marine archeological finds; 350 paintings, 600 maps, and over 15000 photographs.

The Stavanger Maritime Museum is located in Old Stavanger on Strandkaien 22. It is open from Tuesday to Sunday from 11 am to 4 pm.

Norwegian Children's Museum

Established in 2001, this museum focuses on the history of childhood and children's culture. It was originally a private foundation but opened its doors to the public at the turn of the millennium.

There are a number of exhibitions – some continually changing – and play environments that would be of special interest to children. Exhibitions include the Fairytale Castle, Anything For The Children, Toys Tell, and The Historical Games Park, to name a few.

The museum is located to the south of the Breiavatnet Lake on Musegt 16. It is open from Tuesday to Sunday from 11 am to 4 pm.

Stavanger Art Museum

This museum has art collections from the 19th century to the contemporary times. It originally started as the Stavanger Art Association in 1865. The collections started growing manifold during the 2nd half of the 20th century. In 1990, not only was it renamed as the Rogaland Museum of Fine Arts, the institution transformed from being a mere museum to an art center. It became a part of MUST in 2010 and was given the present name. Today, it is housed in a swanky contemporary styled building with an exhibition space of over 2000 sq m featuring over 2000 works of art. Artists featured in the collections include Edvard Munch, Olaf Lange, Kitty Kielland, and Lars Hertervig.

The museum is located about 3 km southwest of the city center beside the beautiful Lake Mosvatnet. It is open from Tuesday to Sunday from 11 am to 4 pm.

Stavanger Museum of Natural History

This wing of the museum is one of the first to be a part of the MUST. Local fauna, along with exotic mammals and birds donated by travelers and sailors, constituted the initial collection of this museum. The basement section of the museum still has some of its oldest collections. There are different sections for mammals and birds. Some of the interesting yet quirky exhibits include chicken with 4 legs, and an actual foot from a mummy!

The museum is located about a km south of Breiavatnet Lake on Musegt 16. It is open from Tuesday to Sunday from 11 am to 4 pm.

Ledaal

The Ledaal is a museum, a royal residence, and a venue for many official functions. It was originally built as the summer residence of the wealthy Kielland family, back in the early 19th century. A visit to this mansion gives a sense of nobility during 19th century Norway. The rich furnishings, elegant décor, and expensive housewares reflect the life and style of the family. The exhibits are laid out over 3 floors. The building and its adjacent park is a national trust. Ledaal is located in southwest Stavanger and is open to the public every Sunday from noon until 4 pm.

Breidablikk

This beautiful residential mansion was built in 1881 for shipping magnate Lars Berensen. This stunning and well preserved house was built in a Swiss architectural style and has Gothic and Romantic influences. The interior of this mansion is considered one of the best preserved. The expensive furniture – in Rococo, Baroque, Gothic, and contemporary styles - reflect the wealth of Lars. The adjacent park with its English landscaping and exotic trees is an attraction in itself. The Breidablikk is located just south of the Ledaal and should not be missed if in that area. It is open to the public every Sunday from noon until 4 pm.

Utstein Monastery

Located in Klosteroy, about a 30 minute drive from Stavanger, this is the only preserved medieval monastery in Norway. The monastery was built in the mid 13th century and got its present look after some renovations and alterations in the mid 18th century. The monastery is set amidst a very scenic setting which itself warrants a visit to this place. The church, monastic estate, refectory, garden, wine cellar, and the library set up a fantastic view. The Fjoloy Lighthouse and the Fjoloy Fort is just a short drive away. It is open on Sundays from 12 noon to 5 pm.

Stavanger Museum of Cultural History

This is another museum housed in the main museum building in Musegt 16. It focuses on the history of Stavanger – from its founding 1125 until 1995. Human models, ethnographic collections, historic artifacts, and various audio-visual exhibits make the visit exciting for children and adults alike.

The Printing Museum is closed to the public presently, and the School Museum is open only by appointment and is aimed at school children.

Broken Column

With 23 iron statues spread all across the city, this is one of the most innovative and interesting art projects in Norway. It is the brainchild of British sculptor Antony Gormley. The 23 sandblasted iron statues are cast in the shape of the artist's body. The height of every statue is 1.95 m – that of the artist. These statues are placed in an imaginary column where each following statue is at an altitude 1.95 m lower than the previous one. The highest statue is on the Stavanger Art Museum and the lowest is at 1.23 m below sea level at the harbor! All the statues are placed facing north towards the sea. If you have some free time and do not mind walking around Old Stavanger and the city center, try and see if you can locate all the statues. A list of all the statues along with the location and the altitude can be found at -
http://gardkarlsen.com/broken_column.htm.

The Geopark & Norwegian Petroleum Museum

The Geopark is a miniature oil and gas field model complete with a colorful landscape. The model – built on an 1:1500 ratio – reconstructed the exact strata of the Troll oil base that lies below the surface. Designed by architects Helen and Hard, the Geopark transformed an abandoned site into a playground for kids. There are facilities for skating, sand volleyball, climbing, and graffiti art. The site is also used for concerts and various other performances.

The Petroleum Museum exhibits how gas and oil are produced and used in our everyday lives. With some original tools, models, and audio-video presentations the museum creates a learning experience which is exciting for visitors of all ages. It also has a 3D movie theater. The Petroleum Museum is located on the harbor area on the Blue Promenade. Exhibits in the museum include the Oil Well Drill Bit, A Nation of Seafarers, Collection of Models, A Universe Below, Safety Training, Escape Chute, The North Sea Divers, Taking a Journey Offshore, and Kid's Corner, to name a few. It is open every day from 10 am to 7 pm.

Flor & Fjaere Nature Park

Located in the Sor-Hidle area of Stavanger, the Flor & Fjaere Nature Park is one of most beautifully landscaped public parks in the city.

The park is full of exotic plants, palm trees, colorful flowers, and is set up in the backdrop of the sea. It has a restaurant that serves delicious international cuisine and a variety of local seafood. The park can be reached by a 20 minute boat trip through the picturesque local fjord. If you are having a couple of hours in hand and want to experience the beauty of the fjord coupled with some great food, this is surely the place to visit.

Escape to Nature

Stavanger in itself is a city that captivates its visitors with its scenic beauty. However, hardcore nature lovers may want to venture out of the city to experience and enjoy the Norwegian landscape which is both unique and scenic.

One of the distinct features of the landscape is the fjords – the glacial cliffs with intermittent water bodies. The Lysefjord in the Stavanger region is one of the most beautiful fjords stretching nearly 42 km and having cliffs that rise almost vertically for 1000 m. The fjord cruise is a good way to enjoy these fjords.

Stavanger may not be the most popular beach town but it does have a few beaches which are known for their clear water and great views.

Solastranden is popular not only for swimming but also for kiting, surfing, and of course, sun bathing. The Godalen Badeplass can be accessed through the Ostre Ring. Although not exactly a beach in every term, it is a popular bathing area and has a number of facilities like children's playground and barbeque zones. The Mollebukta – with the Swords in Stone monument – has a sandy beach that is a popular retreat in the summer months. The Vaulen Beach is adjacent to some of the popular hiking trails of Stavanger. It is equipped with toilets and handicap facilities.

Another popular nature attraction is the Manafossen Waterfall. With a free fall of 92 m, it is the highest in Rogaland County and the 9th highest in Norway. The waterfall is a protected site and can be reached through a short hike.

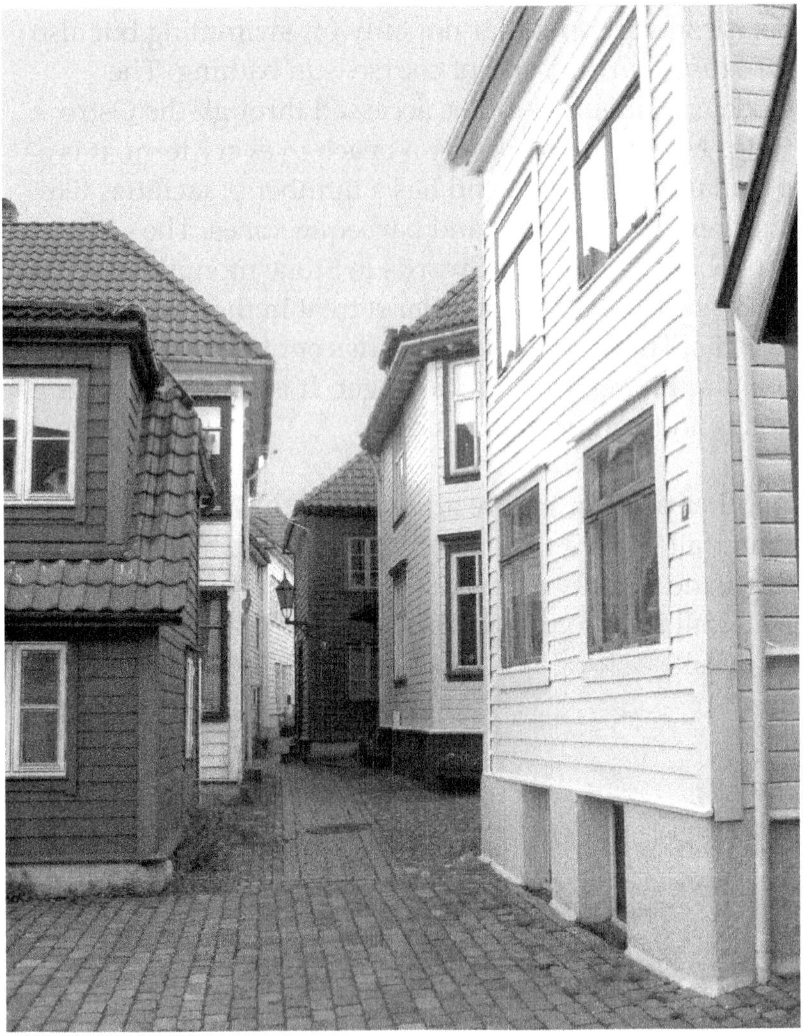

Recommendations for the Budget Traveller

Places to Stay

Skansen Hotel

Skansegt 7
4006 Stavanger
Tel: 47 51 938 500
http://www.skansenhotel.no/indexE.htm

The Skansen is a 2 star hotel located near the northern tip of the city center. It is located within walking distance from most of the popular attractions in the city. This small hotel has a warm personal feel to it making it popular with guests who are looking for a very cozy atmosphere. This non-smoking property has a terrace, 24 hr front desk, and facilities for disabled guests. It has free Wi-Fi and an onsite bar. The hotel is closed during Christmas and Easter.

The ensuite rooms have all basic facilities and are equipped with comfortable beds and TV. Room rates start from NOK 770 and include breakfast.

Victoria Hotel

Skansgt 1
4006 Stavanger
Tel: 47 51 86 7000
http://www.victoria-hotel.no/

This is a 4 star hotel located at a street corner near the cruise ship pier at the city center. Facilities of this non smoking property include 24 hr front desk, concierge service, room service, and free Wi-Fi. Pets are allowed. There is an onsite bar and restaurant.

The 107 ensuite rooms have LCD TV, mini bar, telephone, one arm chair, and free bottled water. Room rates start from NOK 555 per person.

Best Western Havly

Valberggt 1
4006 Stavanger
Tel: 47 51 93 9000
http://www.bestwestern.no/

This 3 star hotel is located near the railway station and the popular shopping streets of Stavanger. This 100% smoke-free hotel's facilities include 24 hr front desk, free Wi-Fi, ice vending machine, fax and photocopier, safe deposit box, elevator, and free newspaper.

The ensuite rooms are equipped with cable TV, ironing board, work area, hairdryer, coffee maker, and telephone. Room rates start from NOK 700 and include breakfast.

First Hotel Alstor

Tjensvollveien 31
Stavanger 4021
Tel: 47 52 04 4000
http://www.firsthotels.no/Vare-Hotell/Hotell-i-Norge/Stavanger/First-Hotel-Alstor/

This is a 3 star hotel located just 100 m from the Stavanger Art Museum. This small but cozy hotel has non-smoking rooms, family rooms, free parking, 24 hr reception, free Wi-Fi, and room service. Pets are allowed. It has an onsite restaurant and bar.

The elegantly decorated ensuite rooms have all the basic modern facilities. Some of the rooms come with a balcony. Room rates start from NOK 630.

Radisson Blu Royal

Lokkeveien 26, 4002 Stavanger
Tel: 47 51 76 6000
http://www.radissonblu.com/royalhotel-stavanger

This 4 star hotel is located immediately west to the Stavanger Old Town.

This non smoking property has facilities for disabled guests, 24 hr reception, room service, and free Wi-Fi. Currency exchange and bicycle rental are available to the guests. The hotel has an indoor pool. There is an onsite restaurant and bar.

The comfortable and spacious ensuite rooms have cable TV, safe deposit box, direct dial telephone, and coffee maker. Room rates start from NOK 956 and include breakfast.

Places to Eat

Flor & Fjaere Nature Park

Skagenkaien 35-37
4006 Stavanger
https://florogfjare.no/english#restaurant

Set amidst a picturesque landscaped garden with exotic trees and plants, this is a place to enjoy international and local cuisine amidst the beauty of nature. The menu is dominated by Italian dishes and local seafood preparations. It is open on all days except Sundays and can be reached by a scenic 20 minute boat ride. Dishes include Hidlefjord Fish Soup, Slow roasted trout with chilli and blood oranges, South African chicken curry, Fresh pasta with wild rocket, and pork belly with fried spinach.

Big Horn

http://www.bighorn.no/restauranter/meny/Stavanger/221

This is part of a chain of restaurants that serves a variety of local and international cuisine – including American fast food. Starters include chicken wings, onion rings, grilled lamb, salad, and garlic bread. They serve a wide variety of steaks and burgers. Desserts include a variety of ice creams, sorbet, cake, and fruits. A 3 to 4 course meal with starter and dessert would cost around NOK 500.

Bevaremegvel

Breigata 5
4006 Stavanger
Tel: 47 51 84 38 60
http://www.herlige-stavanger.no/bevaremegvel/

This cozy restaurant is located in Skagen, on the street that runs behind the Vagen harbor street with all the bars and the cafes. The restaurant is popular for its atmosphere, great food, and coffee. It serves a wide variety ranging from sandwiches and to full course dinners. The main course is dominated by meat dishes – chicken, duck, pork, and veal, so non-vegetarians would have a wide choice. It is open from 11 am to late hours.

Harbour Café

Skagen 27, 4006 Stavanger
Tel: 47 51 5999 70
http://www.harbourbowl.no/

Located on a cobbled street in the harbor area, this café serves a wide range of international and American fast food. Medium price range, great views, and of course, delicious food, has made this café popular with many locals. Dishes include grilled scallops, garlic bread with cheese, American hot wings, pepper steak, Bourbon steak, chicken fajitas, pasta, sandwiches, burgers, and desserts – including cheesecakes and brownies. A meal for one would cost around NOK 250.

Gaffel & Karaffel

Ovreholmegate 20, 4006 Stavanger
Tel: 47 51 86 41 58
http://gaffelogkaraffel.no/

Located midway between the Vagen harbor and the Petroleum Museum, this is a high-end restaurant for those who are looking for a romantic dinner or looking to splurge. It specializes in international cuisine with a wide variety of fish and meat dishes. The restaurant has 100 covers and is open for dinners from Wednesday to Saturday. Dishes include a variety of salads, grilled poussin, poached cod, parmesan baked potatoes, grilled pork chop, and glazed baby back ribs. A 3-course meal would cost about NOK 500.

Places to Shop

Bjork Birch

http://www.bjork-birch.no/

Located on Nygaten, this is one of the best places to buy Norwegian gifts. This exclusive gift shop sells a variety of gift items including health and food products, minerals and rocks, locally made jam and juice, and tourist t-shirts. It also sells magnets, key chains, and postcards.

Stavanger Glassblasseri

http://www.stavangerglass.no/

The store sells a variety of beautiful glass products created by glass-artist Trine Sundt. From goblets and plates to room decorations, the store has a wide range of designs that make a wonderful souvenir from Stavanger. The store is open Tuesday to Friday from 10 am to 4 pm. It has shortened hours on Saturdays and is closed on Sundays.

Ullform

http://www.ullform.no/

This is the ideal store to visit if you are looking to buy felt products to decorate your home. The store sells silk, wool, and felting equipments. Products sold include pillow covers, hats, shoes, handkerchiefs, and even raw sheets of silk and yarn. Be it for personal use or for gifting, Ullform warrants a visit if you are shopping in Stavanger.

Kvadrat

http://www.kvadrat.no/

This is not only the largest shopping center in Stavanger but also one of the largest in Norway with over 160 stores and restaurants, a pharmacy, a bank, a post office, a tourist office, a wine store, and a playground! This is certainly the place to visit if you are looking to buy everything under one roof.

Fish Market

http://fisketorget-stavanger.no/

If you are a fish lover, then the fish market is a must-visit place. You may not be buying or cooking any fish during your trip to Stavanger, but just to see so many varieties of fish in one market is an experience not to miss.

Along with the regular catches like shrimps and crabs, the fish market also sells exclusive fresh catches like scallops, lobsters, and oysters. If the fresh catches tickle your taste buds, there is an adjacent restaurant where not only can you taste some fresh cooked seafood; you can also get tips from the chefs how to prepare those dishes.